SimplyHealthful

Pizzas
and
Calzones

Simply Healthful

Pizzas
and
Calzones

Delicious New Low-Fat Recipes

By David Ricketts & Susan McQuillan
Photography by Steven Mark Needham

CHAPTERS™

CHAPTERS PUBLISHING LTD., SHELBURNE, VERMONT 05482

Published by
Chapters Publishing Ltd.
2085 Shelburne Road
Shelburne, Vermont 05482

Library of Congress Cataloging-in-Publication Data

Ricketts, David.
    Simply healthful pizzas and calzones : delicious new low-fat recipes
by David Ricketts & Susan McQuillan;
photography by Steven Mark Needham.
        p. cm. — (Simply healthful series)
Includes index.
ISBN 1-881527-34-4
1. Pizza. 2. Calzone. I. McQuillan, Susan. II. Title. III. Series.
TX770.P58R53   1994
641.8'24—dc20   93-45013

Printed and bound in Canada by
Friesen Printers
Altona, Manitoba

Designed by Eugenie Seidenberg Delaney
Cover design by Susan McClellan

10 9 8 7 6 5 4 3 2

About the Authors

DAVID RICKETTS AND SUSAN MCQUILLAN wrote *Simply Healthful Fish*. David Ricketts is a contributing food editor for *Family Circle Magazine* and food editor for the Great American Baking series. Susan McQuillan is a food and nutrition editor at *American Health* magazine and a registered dietitian. She is a frequent contributor to *Family Circle*, *Cooking Light* and other magazines.

Special Thanks

IRENE MCQUILLAN TASTED our very first pizza and contributed lots of ideas throughout. Joyce Rambo and Tom Reynolds tasted almost everything and offered sage comments after each and every bite. Sue Hohl and Dan Yaccarino brought their appetites downtown on a regular basis, while Jill Connors and Joe Cooper helped us run off the calories that can add up even with low-fat recipes. A special thanks to Craig Hohl for computer support, kitchen assistance and nap advice. Joseph Oliveri and Alton McCloud inspired exciting recipes and gave helpful criticism. During the March blizzard of 1992, Tom Votta introduced us to the pizza in Boston's Italian North End. Anne Clune, a friend of many years, gave us so many ideas we couldn't fit them all into one book.

Contents

Introduction

PROBABLY THE GREATEST REWARD of writing any cookbook is the chance to cook and share food with family and friends. We found this especially true whenever we baked pizzas and calzones. In our experience, no one ever passes up an invitation to a pizza party.

Sitting around the dining table or lounging on the floor, guests gobbled up our breadstuffs and offered their own suggestions for improving recipes as well as for creating new ones. From them, we gathered inspiration for some of our favorites: Black Bean Pizza, an easy-to-assemble combination of tomato, black beans and mozzarella and Monterey Jack cheeses sprinkled with fresh cilantro; a white pizza with onions and three cheeses; a crostini topping of artichoke hearts, tomato and ripe olives seasoned with cumin and paprika; and a deliciously gooey Monterey-Mushroom Calzone, filled with wild mushrooms and mozzarella and Jack cheeses.

Pizza, calzones and crostini are, of course, especially suited to informal gatherings. They are essentially similar: pizza, flat bread dough with a topping; calzones, turnovers with savory fillings; and crostini, which are nothing more than toasts with a topping. Hand-held, like a sandwich, they rarely require utensils. Calzones or slices of pizza travel well: on a road trip, to the office, to a potluck party or to a picnic. And once they get there, they can be anything: appetizer, nibble, lunch, dinner, snack or sometimes even dessert. At our parties, we often served samples of each, beginning with, for example, caramelized-onion-topped crostini as an appetizer, moving on to calzones stuffed with chicken and sun-dried tomatoes, and concluding with a dessertlike apple and cheese pizza, which pairs the natural sweetness of apple with the sharpness of blue cheese.

Because they are like sandwiches, pizzas, calzones and crostini accommodate a wide array of toppings and fillings, from simple, traditional Italian ones like sausage and pepper, or tomato, mozzarella and fresh basil to unexpected but equally delicious combinations: shrimp and feta cheese or chili powder, tomato and corn.

Our goal was to make each recipe low in fat, high in flavor and simple to prepare. For all their versatility, traditional pizzas and calzones have one disadvantage: the dough can be time-consuming to make from scratch. We developed yeast doughs that take less than 15 minutes to prepare and can be baked without a rising. In fact, most of the tasters at our parties couldn't tell the difference between risen and unrisen dough, and some even preferred the unrisen version. To save even more time, the doughs can be made in several batches and refrigerated or frozen for future use.

The toppings and fillings are also quick to assemble, and they can be used interchangeably. The Ratatouille and Wild Mushroom Pizza toppings, for example, can just as easily fill a calzone or top a crostini toast. The filling for Spinach and Ricotta Calzones With Raisins sits equally well on a slice of pizza or a crostini. The tomato and broccoli crostini topping complements either a pizza or a calzone.

Our pizzas, calzones and crostini have a healthful advantage over traditional varieties: they are lower in fat. Unlike the typical pie from your local pizzeria, our thin-crust, crispy pizzas won't leak oil onto your lap while you're eating them. High-fat cheeses have been kept to a minimum and are mixed with reduced-fat cheeses. While other pizzas may conceal 8 to 15 grams of fat per slice, ours generally contain only 5 or 6 grams per slice. We have learned that more isn't always better, so we don't overload the pies or crostini with heavy toppings or overstuff the calzones with dense fillings. The emphasis is on fresh vegetables and clean, individual flavors.

Cheese, Please

WITH FEW EXCEPTIONS, our recipes for pizzas, calzones and crostini use lots of cheese. To keep the recipes in line with a low-fat approach to eating, we've used a variety of reduced-fat and full-fat cheese combinations.

Our favorite is reduced-fat mozzarella cheese, with one-half to two-thirds less fat than whole-milk mozzarella. You'll find it in many of the recipes, combined with smaller amounts of more flavorful, often higher-fat cheeses.

We tried to use nonfat mozzarella as well, but found that it melted oddly and then virtually disappeared somewhere in the baking process. (No wonder it contributes fewer calories!) As a result, we've stayed with the reduced-fat varieties. Since reduced-fat cheeses are usually not aged as long as their full-fat counterparts, they are milder in flavor, with a higher moisture content that results in different cooking properties. However, we found that most reduced-fat cheeses work perfectly well on pizzas and in calzones, particularly when combined with small amounts of more flavorful, full-fat cheeses.

None of the cheese combinations used in the recipes in this book are carved in stone. You can use any mixture you like. The secret is to use reduced-fat cheeses together with higher-fat varieties so that you cut back on total fat without giving up favorite flavors.

We have the Wisconsin Milk Marketing Board, and in particular Linda Funk and Patrick Geoghegan, to thank for telling us everything we needed to know about cheese, and more. With their help, we compiled the following list of cheese blends and compatible pizza toppings to guide you in modifying our recipes with your choice of cheese and to create pizzas of your own. To keep the fat down, we recommend that at least one of the cheeses in any of the following mixtures be a reduced-fat variety. (Reduced-fat mozzarella, which is included in all these combinations, is probably the most commonly available.) Your blend should contain a higher proportion of reduced-fat cheese, with smaller amounts of full-fat cheeses added for more flavor.

Sharp Cheddar, Mozzarella and Provolone. This mixture works well on an all-cheese pizza (with or without sauce), or with broccoli, cauliflower or fresh tomato topping. Try it also with a lightly seasoned lean ground meat or poultry topping.

Fontina, Gruyère and Mozzarella. Anything you would use for dipping into fondue goes well with these cheeses: meat, chicken, poultry or shrimp. Pair this blend with lightly sautéed or caramelized onions, or use it to make a white, cheese-only pizza.

Fresh Goat Cheese and Mozzarella. If you like goat cheese, use it to top any vegetable pizza. It also marries well with the flavors of fresh herbs, such as basil and oregano, and condiments like black olives and bits of sun-dried tomatoes.

Mozzarella, Brick and Blue. Mild, buttery brick cheese can carry the strong flavor of a crumbly blue. Try this combination on a fruit pizza, a seafood pie or a salad pizza, or with a mild-flavored vegetable topping, such as steamed summer squash.

Smoked Gouda and Mozzarella. Any smoked cheese combination can be used alone as a topping for cheese pizza. Or try with a mushroom or shredded cooked chicken topping.

Monterey Jack, Cheddar and Mozzarella. This is a classic combination for Tex-Mex-style pizzas made with beans and/or salsa.

Working the Dough

OUR BASIC YEAST DOUGH for pizza and the one for calzones are easy to work with, responding well to 5 to 10 minutes of kneading with little additional flour necessary. And the two doughs are interchangeable. If you are really in a rush, you can omit the risings, and in that case, the dough will be ready to use in about 15 minutes. For one rising, add an additional hour, and for the second rising, another 30 minutes.

Quick-rising yeast, which is not available everywhere, can reduce rising time by one-third to one-half. If you do not plan to give the dough a rise, using quick-rising yeast is pointless. If you do decide to use it, follow the directions on the package, since the method differs from that of ordinary yeast.

FLOURS AND FLAVORS

You can substitute whole-wheat flour for part of the white for a nuttier, sweet-tasting crust with a "darker" flavor. For a more breadlike and slightly more chewy crust, substitute bread flour for the white.

Flavored crusts introduce a range of subtle or sometimes not-so-subtle flavor combinations as well as visual variations. To the flour, add a teaspoon or up to a tablespoon of a dried herb or spice, such as oregano, rosemary, basil, cracked black pepper, chili powder or coriander. Chopped scallions, black olives and roasted red peppers are other crust additions you might consider.

Another good flavor trick is to brush the crust with a tablespoon of bottled nonfat vinaigrette salad dressing before prebaking. Or experiment with different nonfat flavored dressings if they seem a natural match for the topping, such as Ranch Dressing with chicken or French with tomato and onion.

Easy Crusts

If you have a hankering for pizza, but don't want to deal with our easy-to-make-from-scratch crust, there are numerous alternatives for practically any occasion, whether it be dinner or a party. Ready-to-top, premade bread pizza crusts, packaged in cellophane and available in the supermarket, come in a large and a small size. Layer on one of our toppings or your own impromptu combination, and bake according to the package directions.

English muffins have long been popular for individual, quick pizzas. Lightly toast the muffin first for extra crispness. Then add the topping and give the muffin another toasting to heat everything through. You can do the same thing with pita pockets split in half.

The Scandinavian flatbreads and even matzos make a crunchy, no-fuss base for a party pizza hors d'oeuvre.

Although refrigerated pizza and bread doughs do save a step or two, once you've made our doughs from scratch a few times, we think you'll much prefer their taste and texture.

Pizzas

ESSENTIALLY, PIZZA is nothing more than a circle of thin bread, covered with a topping and baked. The Italian word *pizza*, loosely translated, means "flattened" or "pie."

Pizza is reputed to have Greco-Roman roots. Theories about its origins are mostly anecdotal, but pizza as we know it probably developed in Naples, where *pizzerie* shops became quite common by the mideighteenth century. Today, there are thought to be about 5,000 pizza ovens in this same city.

Initially a combination of inexpensive ingredients meant for simple daily nourishment and to be eaten out of hand, the pizza has been transformed over the last 10 years in this country into something highly creative and often idiosyncratic. Choices here range from the basic Tomato with Mozzarella and Basil to more venturesome combinations like Salad Pizza, Shrimp Pizza With Feta, Wild Mushroom Pizza and a Mexican pizza with bottled salsa as the sauce.

Most of these pizzas are delicious hot from the oven and are also good at room temperature. Leftovers from the refrigerator make great breakfast food as well as instant snacks.

Our recipes make 12-inch rounds, but you can shape square, rectangular or individual mini pizzas if you prefer. One thing is sure, however: once you make a few pizzas from scratch, you'll discover it's no bother at all to throw one together, using whatever leftovers you have hiding in your refrigerator.

Pizza Equipment

Pizza Pans: We use all sorts of pans for baking pizzas: 12-inch rounds in dark or black steel; shiny aluminum pans; flat pans with a lip or a rippled edge; jelly-roll pans; ordinary baking sheets; round layer cake pans; and cast-iron skillets. Since the crispness of our crust comes from prebaking, the type of baking pan or baking sheet you select is less important than in recipes where prebaking is not called for. Almost any pan you have in your cupboards will do. For cutting pizza, we recommend transferring it to a cutting surface to avoid scratching the pan.

Pizza Baking Stones and Unglazed Tiles: Many people wouldn't attempt pizza without these, but we think the lengthy preheating wastes energy and makes the kitchen even more uncomfortable on a warm day. The stones do duplicate the intense, dry heat of a pizza oven, contributing to even browning and a crisp crust. Unglazed quarry tiles suitable for baking can be found in home-improvement centers or tile shops, and baking stones can be found in cookware shops and some hardware stores.

Cheese Grater: We avoid using a food processor for grating cheese, since it tends to "mush" the cheese and make it lumpy, resulting in uneven melting. An old-fashioned, sturdy, upright grater with a handle is the best bet. Use the large holes.

Marble Slab: Granted, this may be seem an extravagance, especially if you're short on counter space. But its cool surface makes working with the dough much simpler since there's less sticking and easier cleanup. As a bonus, you may discover you're apt to make not only pizzas and calzones more frequently but also pie crusts—if you leave the marble slab out on the counter rather than hauling it in and out of the cupboard.

Dough Scraper: Available in hard plastic or as a stainless-steel blade with a wooden handle, dough scrapers make working with dough and cleaning surfaces much easier.

Food Processor: If you're making several batches of pizza dough (or calzone dough), a food processor can speed things up a bit. To us, it seems more trouble than it's worth. Our pizza and calzone doughs are so easy to work with that after you try a few recipes, you'll find their preparation almost as quick by hand. Working the dough manually also gives you the chance to get the feel of the dough as it moves from its wet, sticky stage to the smooth, responsive ball—a sensuous experience. For the Food Processor Method, see Basic Pizza Dough, page 20.

Rolling Pin: Our doughs are easy to stretch and pat out onto the pan. If you're more comfortable with a rolling pin, then by all means use one.

Cutting Wheel: If you don't already have one, we would strongly recommend purchasing it. The better constructed it is, the longer it will last. Look for a sturdy handle with a blade guard and a 3-to-3½-inch wheel, beveled on one side to create a sharp cutting edge.

For fast preparation, you can use this dough without waiting for it to rise. Just let it rest for 10 minutes after the kneading in Step 2, then pat it out into the shape specified in the recipe (see Shaping the Dough, page 22). Or if you like, you can give the dough just one rising rather than two; then punch it down and let rest for 10 minutes.

Surprisingly, there is not a huge difference between the no-rise crust and the crust with risings. The latter is slightly more puffy with a breadier texture, but the no-rise version can easily pass for the risen. The secret is the initial prebaking of the crust at a high heat, which causes even the no-rise version to "explode" and puff into a crisp base.

If a recipe calls for one 12-inch pizza crust, make the entire recipe and freeze the half you don't need. For refrigerating and freezing the dough, see the instructions on page 21.

Basic Pizza Dough

1   envelope (2½ teaspoons) active dry yeast
1   teaspoon sugar
1   cup lukewarm water (95-105 degrees F)
3   cups unbleached all-purpose flour, plus extra for kneading
¼   teaspoon salt
1   teaspoon olive oil
    Vegetable oil for coating bowl

MAKING DOUGH

1. Dissolve yeast and sugar in lukewarm water in 1-cup glass measure. Let stand until foamy, 5 to 10 minutes.

2. **Hand method:** Combine flour and salt in large bowl. Make well in center of flour. Pour yeast mixture and olive oil into well. Stir in flour from bowl with your hand or large spoon to make soft dough.

Food Processor Method: Combine flour and salt in processor. Then, with motor running, add yeast mixture and oil through feed tube and continue to process just until dough comes together in wet, sticky mass.

3. Turn dough out onto lightly floured work surface. Knead until smooth and elastic, 5 to 10 minutes, adding a little flour as needed to prevent sticking. (If you wish, at this point you can let dough rest for 10 minutes, omit risings, shape dough and proceed with a recipe. For instructions on shaping dough, see page 22.)

RISING DOUGH

4. Wash and dry large bowl and coat very lightly with vegetable oil. Return dough to bowl and turn to coat top. Cover with damp dish towel. Let rise in warm place (75 degrees F), away from drafts, until doubled in size, about 1 hour.

5. Punch down dough. Turn dough out onto work surface and knead for 2 minutes. Return dough to bowl. Cover and let rise in warm place (75 degrees F), away from drafts, for 30 minutes.

6. Punch down dough. Divide in half. Shape half into pizza (see page 22) and store other half.

REFRIGERATING DOUGH

Dough can be refrigerated before first rise, or punched down after first rise and then refrigerated. (Label dough so you remember at what point it was refrigerated.) Place dough in plastic bag, leaving a little room for expansion, seal tightly and refrigerate for up to 3 days. Let come to room temperature before using as directed in recipe.

FREEZING DOUGH

Dough can be frozen before first rise, or punched down after first rise and then frozen. Lightly dust dough with flour, wrap tightly in plastic wrap and slip into freezer-proof plastic bag. Seal, label and freeze for up to 1 month. To use, thaw in refrigerator 12 hours or overnight. Let come to room temperature before using as directed in recipe.

Makes enough dough for two 12-inch pizza crusts (8 slices each).

90 CALORIES PER SLICE OF CRUST: 3 G PROTEIN; 1 G FAT; 18 G CARBOHYDRATE; 34 MG SODIUM; 0 MG CHOLESTEROL.

WHOLE-WHEAT PIZZA DOUGH:

Prepare Basic Pizza Dough, using 2 cups whole-wheat flour and 1 cup unbleached white all-purpose flour. For a lighter crust, substitute only 1 cup whole-wheat flour, or even just ½ cup.

84 CALORIES PER SLICE OF CRUST: 3 G PROTEIN; 1 G FAT; 17 G CARBOHYDRATE; 35 MG SODIUM; 0 MG CHOLESTEROL.

Shaping the Dough

HAND-STRETCHING METHOD

This is the method we prefer: it produces a tender crust that puffs up especially well around the edges, creating a homey, rustic-looking pie. The rolling-pin method (see below) usually flattens out the air bubbles in the dough and produces a denser crust, less likely to "puff."

If you haven't worked with pizza dough before, just remember, it's pretty durable—you really can't mistreat it as you stretch it. So have no fear. The more frequently you make pizza, the more you will automatically know the feel of the dough, and your hands will quickly stretch it to its proper size, without a second thought. You can try tossing the dough in the air and catching it on your fists, but we think that technique is best left for the show in pizzeria windows. Our method is much easier and ensures the dough will stay off the floor.

Flatten dough out into a disk. Then pick it up in both hands, holding it along one edge, and turn it as you would a steering wheel.

Stretch dough between your hands as you turn it. When dough is about 10 inches in diameter (for 12-inch pizza) and somewhere between ⅛ and ¼ inch thick, plop it down on a pizza pan that has been lightly dusted with yellow cornmeal. If dough has been stretched too thin and is torn, don't worry. Just push the tears together to patch.

To fit dough in pan, press it out with your fingers to edge of pan, making ridge around outside so dough will puff higher around edge than in center when baked. It is not necessary for dough to fit neatly. In fact, the more uneven, the more attractive the final result. *If at any time dough seems too elastic to work with and won't stretch out easily, let it rest for 5 minutes or so.*

ROLLING-PIN METHOD

If you're not a hand-stretcher, for whatever reasons, by all means use the rolling pin. The pizza will still be delicious. Flatten dough into a disk with your hand. Then roll it out, working from center to edge, rolling in one motion, without rolling back. Turn dough a quarter turn as you roll, so circle expands evenly. If dough becomes too elastic as you roll, let it rest for 5 minutes. When done, transfer it to pan and proceed as in hand-stretching method.

Basic Chunky Tomato Sauce

1   teaspoon olive oil
1   small onion, chopped
2   cloves garlic, finely chopped
1   can (28 ounces) Italian-style plum tomatoes, coarsely chopped, with juice
½   teaspoon salt
¼   teaspoon freshly ground black pepper

1. Lightly coat large nonstick skillet with olive oil. Heat over medium heat. Add onion; sauté until softened, about 5 minutes. Add garlic; sauté 1 minute.

2. Add tomatoes with their juice. Cook over medium heat, stirring occasionally, until thickened, about 30 minutes. Stir in salt and pepper. Use sauce immediately, or cool and then refrigerate, covered, for up to 4 days or freeze for up to 1 month.

Makes about 2 cups (1 cup is enough for one 12-inch pizza).

15 CALORIES PER 2 TABLESPOONS: 1 G PROTEIN; 0 G FAT; 3 G CARBOHYDRATE; 148 MG SODIUM; 0 MG CHOLESTEROL.

ROASTED RED PEPPER VARIATION:
Drain one 7½-ounce jar roasted red peppers in a sieve. Rinse under cold water. Gently dry on paper towels. Puree in blender or food processor. Stir pepper puree into tomato sauce.

19 CALORIES PER 2 TABLESPOONS: 1 G PROTEIN; 0 G FAT; 4 G CARBOHYDRATE; 148 MG SODIUM; 0 MG CHOLESTEROL.

Feel free to season this sauce to suit your own desires—with oregano, basil, fennel seeds, anchovy paste or more garlic.

Tomato Pizza With Mozzarella and Basil

1	recipe Whole-Wheat Pizza Dough (page 21)
	Yellow cornmeal for skillet
¼	pound reduced-fat mozzarella cheese, shredded (about 1 cup)
3	large ripe tomatoes (about 1½ pounds), sliced ¼ inch thick
2	ounces grated Parmesan cheese (about ⅔ cup)
¼	cup chopped fresh basil

1. Prepare Whole-Wheat Pizza Dough, reserving half the dough for another pizza.

2. Preheat oven to 500 degrees F. Place oven rack in lowest position.

3. Sprinkle bottom of 9-inch cast-iron skillet or other heavy oven-proof skillet with a little cornmeal. Spread pizza dough in bottom of skillet.

4. Bake crust on lowest oven rack for 7 minutes, or until lightly browned and crisp.

5. Sprinkle half of mozzarella over prebaked crust, leaving ½-inch border all around. Layer tomatoes over cheese. Sprinkle with remaining mozzarella and Parmesan.

6. Bake for 8 to 12 minutes, or until topping is heated through and edge of crust is browned. Sprinkle with basil. Let stand for 5 minutes before cutting.

Makes 8 slices.

164 CALORIES PER SLICE: 11 G PROTEIN; 5 G FAT; 22 G CARBOHYDRATE; 269 MG SODIUM; 11 MG CHOLESTEROL.

Fresh and Sun-Dried Tomato Pizza With Olives

1	recipe Basic Pizza Dough (page 20)
1	pound ripe plum tomatoes, seeded and diced
	Yellow cornmeal for pizza pan
1	tablespoon chopped dry-pack sun-dried tomatoes (not packed in oil)
¼	cup sliced oil-cured, pitted black olives or sliced canned, drained, rinsed black olives
¼	cup finely chopped fresh basil or 1 teaspoon dried
¼	pound reduced-fat mozzarella cheese, shredded (about 1 cup)

1. Prepare Basic Pizza Dough, reserving half the dough for another pizza.

2. Preheat oven to 500 degrees F. Place oven rack in lowest position.

3. Meanwhile, drain diced fresh tomatoes on a double layer of paper toweling.

4. Sprinkle 12-inch pizza pan with a little cornmeal. Pat dough out evenly in pan, leaving slight edge all around.

5. Bake crust on lowest oven rack for 5 minutes, or until lightly browned and crisp.

6. Toss together fresh tomatoes, sun-dried tomatoes, olives and basil in small bowl. Spread evenly over prebaked crust, leaving ½-inch border all around. Sprinkle evenly with cheese.

7. Bake for 8 to 10 minutes, or until cheese is melted, topping is heated through and edge of crust is browned. Let stand for 5 minutes before cutting.

Makes 8 slices.

140 CALORIES PER SLICE: 8 G PROTEIN; 3 G FAT; 22 G CARBOHYDRATE; 174 MG SODIUM; 5 MG CHOLESTEROL.

White Pizza With Onions

1 recipe Basic Pizza Dough (page 20)
½ cup Basic Chunky Tomato Sauce (page 23)
1 teaspoon olive oil
½ pound yellow onions, halved and thinly sliced
Yellow cornmeal for pizza pan
1 cup reduced-fat ricotta cheese
1 tablespoon finely chopped fresh parsley
½ teaspoon dried basil
Pinch dried mint
2 ounces reduced-fat mozzarella cheese, shredded (about ½ cup)
2 ounces sharp provolone cheese, shredded (about ½ cup)

A pinch of dried mint leaves added to the ricotta wakes up the flavor of this three-cheese pie. For a basic white pizza, omit the onions. This pie can also be topped with olives, roasted peppers, sliced fresh tomatoes or leftover cooked chicken. We like it just as it is, with a crisp vegetable salad on the side.

1. Prepare Basic Pizza Dough, reserving half the dough for another pizza. Prepare Basic Chunky Tomato Sauce.

2. Heat oil in large nonstick skillet over medium heat. Add onions; sauté for 5 minutes, or until softened. Set aside.

3. Preheat oven to 500 degrees F. Place oven rack in lowest position.

4. Sprinkle 12-inch pizza pan with a little cornmeal. Pat dough out evenly in pan, leaving slight edge all around outside. Spread tomato sauce evenly over dough, leaving ½-inch border all around.

5. Bake crust on lowest oven rack for 5 minutes, or until edge is lightly browned and crisp.

6. Combine ricotta cheese, parsley, basil and mint in small bowl. Spread over prebaked crust. Top with cooked onions. Sprinkle evenly with mozzarella and provolone cheeses.

7. Bake for 8 to 10 minutes, or until topping is heated through and edge of crust is browned. Let stand for 5 minutes before cutting.

Makes 8 slices.

196 CALORIES PER SLICE: 11 G PROTEIN; 6 G FAT; 24 G CARBOHYDRATE; 257 MG SODIUM; 17 MG CHOLESTEROL.

Ratatouille Pizza

1   recipe Basic Pizza Dough (page 20)
1   tablespoon olive oil
1   large onion, finely chopped
1   small eggplant (½ pound), cut into 1-inch cubes
1   yellow or red bell pepper, thinly sliced
1   small zucchini (about 6 ounces), halved lengthwise and sliced
      crosswise ¼ inch thick
4   cloves garlic, finely chopped
1   tablespoon chopped mixed fresh herbs, such as thyme, oregano
      and basil, or 1 teaspoon mixed dried herbs or dried Italian
      herb seasoning
½   teaspoon salt
¼   teaspoon crushed red pepper flakes
2   medium-size ripe tomatoes, cored, seeded and coarsely chopped
      Yellow cornmeal for pizza pans
¼   pound provolone cheese, shredded (about 1 cup)
¼   pound reduced-fat mozzarella cheese, shredded (about 1 cup)
2   tablespoons grated Parmesan cheese

1. Prepare Basic Pizza Dough.

2. Heat oil in large nonstick skillet over medium heat. Add onion; sauté 2 minutes. Add eggplant, bell pepper, zucchini, garlic, herbs, salt and red pepper flakes; cook, stirring often, for 5 minutes. Reduce heat to low; cover and cook 30 minutes, stirring occasionally.

3. Add tomatoes; simmer, uncovered, stirring occasionally, for 15 minutes, or until vegetables are tender and liquid has evaporated. Remove from heat and set aside 15 minutes before topping pizza.

4. Preheat oven to 500 degrees F. Place oven rack in lowest position.

5. Sprinkle two 12-inch pizza pans with a little cornmeal. Pat dough out evenly in pans, leaving slight edge all around.

6. Bake crusts on lowest oven rack for 5 minutes, or until lightly browned and crisp.

Here's a good way to use up summer's garden bounty, especially for a party. This recipe makes enough vegetable mixture for two pies, so you can follow the recipe—or use half the pizza dough and make one pizza, and serve the remaining ratatouille mixture as a vegetable side dish at another meal or add vegetable broth and serve it as a stew.

(continued on page 30)

7. Combine provolone, mozzarella and Parmesan cheeses in small bowl.

8. Divide ratatouille mixture between prebaked crusts, spreading evenly and leaving ½-inch border all around. Sprinkle evenly with cheese mixture.

9. Bake for 8 minutes, or until cheese is melted, topping is heated through and edge of crust is browned. Let stand for 5 minutes before cutting.

Makes 16 slices (2 pizzas).

156 CALORIES PER SLICE: 8 G PROTEIN; 4 G FAT; 22 G CARBOHYDRATE; 228 MG SODIUM; 8 MG CHOLESTEROL.

Wild Mushroom Pizza

1   recipe Basic Pizza Dough (page 20)
1   cup (½ recipe) Basic Chunky Tomato Sauce (page 23)
     Yellow cornmeal for pan
2   teaspoons olive oil
¾   pound wild mushrooms or mixture of wild and button
        mushrooms, cleaned, tough stems removed, and caps
        thinly sliced
2   tablespoons balsamic vinegar
1   teaspoon dried leaf thyme
2   ounces reduced-fat mozzarella cheese, shredded (about ½ cup)
3   ounces Taleggio, chopped, or other semisoft cheese, such as
        Muenster or fontina (about ¾ cup)

1. Prepare Basic Pizza Dough, reserving half the dough for another pizza. Prepare Basic Chunky Tomato Sauce.

2. Preheat oven to 500 degrees F. Place oven rack in lowest position.

3. Sprinkle 12-inch pizza pan with a little yellow cornmeal. Pat dough out evenly in pan, leaving slight edge all around.

4. Bake crust on lowest oven rack for 7 minutes, or until lightly browned and crisp.

5. Meanwhile, heat olive oil in large nonstick skillet over medium heat. Add mushrooms; sauté for 3 minutes. Add vinegar and thyme; cook, stirring often, for 8 minutes, or until mushrooms are tender and any liquid has evaporated from skillet.

6. Spread tomato sauce evenly over prebaked crust, leaving ½-inch border all around. Top with mushrooms. Sprinkle evenly with mozzarella and Taleggio cheeses.

7. Bake for 8 to 10 minutes, or until cheese is melted, topping is heated through and edge of crust is browned. Let stand for 5 minutes before cutting.

Makes 8 slices.

184 CALORIES PER SLICE: 9 G PROTEIN; 6 G FAT; 25 G CARBOHYDRATE; 285 MG SODIUM; 11 MG CHOLESTEROL.

You can use any assortment of mushrooms on this pie. If budget is a factor, use half common button mushrooms and half of the more exotic mushrooms, such as shiitake, portobello, morels or oyster.

Roasted Three-Pepper Pizza

This pie tastes much richer than it really is. The peppers can be roasted earlier in the day or even a day ahead, and you can use just one kind of pepper, if you prefer. To save more time, drain a 7-ounce jar of roasted red peppers, pat dry with paper towels, and substitute them for the roasted fresh. The Gruyère and Parmesan make a sharp-tasting combination. Serve eight small individual pizzas for a first course, or about twelve 3-inch-wide pizzas for an appetizer.

1	recipe Basic Pizza Dough (page 20)
½	cup Basic Chunky Tomato Sauce (page 23)
1	red bell pepper
1	yellow bell pepper
1	green bell pepper
2	ounces reduced-fat mozzarella cheese, shredded (about ½ cup)
2	ounces Gruyère cheese, shredded (about ½ cup)
1	tablespoon grated Parmesan cheese
	Yellow cornmeal for pizza pan
½	small red onion, halved and thinly sliced crosswise

1. Prepare Basic Pizza Dough, reserving half the dough for another pizza. Prepare Basic Chunky Tomato Sauce.

2. Preheat broiler. Broil peppers on broiler-pan rack 4 inches from heat, turning frequently, until blackened on all sides, about 20 minutes. Transfer peppers to paper bag and close. When cool enough to handle, peel off blackened skins. Rinse, if necessary, to remove any stubborn skins. Blot dry. Cut peppers in half, and remove stem and seeds. Cut peppers into small squares. Reserve. Reduce oven temperature to 500 degrees F. Place oven rack in lowest position.

3. Combine mozzarella, Gruyère and Parmesan cheeses in small bowl.

4. Sprinkle 12-inch pizza pan with a little yellow cornmeal. Pat dough out evenly in pan, leaving slight edge all around.

5. Bake crust on lowest oven rack for 5 minutes, or until lightly browned and crisp.

6. Spread tomato sauce evenly over prebaked crust, leaving ½-inch border all around. Sprinkle evenly with cheeses. Arrange peppers over top. Sprinkle with red onion.

7. Bake for 10 to 12 minutes, or until topping is heated through and edge of crust is browned. Let stand for 5 minutes before cutting.

Makes 8 slices.

155 CALORIES PER SLICE: 8 G PROTEIN; 4 G FAT; 22 G CARBOHYDRATE; 194 MG SODIUM; 11 MG CHOLESTEROL.

We love the slightly bitter taste that Italian broccoli rabe lends to this pizza, but if you wish, you can substitute one pound (4 to 5 cups) broccoli florets. Used sliced cherry tomatoes if large tomatoes are out of season.

Broccoli Rabe Pizza With Tomato

1	recipe Basic Pizza Dough (page 20)
	Yellow cornmeal for pizza pan
1½	pounds broccoli rabe, trimmed of thick stems
1	teaspoon olive oil
2-3	cloves garlic, sliced
¼	teaspoon salt
⅛	teaspoon freshly ground black pepper
2	ounces Swiss cheese, shredded (about ½ cup)
2	ounces reduced-fat mozzarella cheese, shredded (about ½ cup)
1	ounce grated Parmesan cheese (about ⅓ cup)
2	medium tomatoes, halved and thinly sliced (½ pound)

1. Prepare Basic Pizza Dough, reserving half the dough for another pizza.

2. Preheat oven to 500 degrees F. Place oven rack in lowest position.

3. Sprinkle 12-inch pizza pan with a little yellow cornmeal. Pat dough out evenly in pan, leaving slight edge all around.

4. Bake crust on lowest oven rack for 5 minutes, or until lightly browned and crisp.

5. Meanwhile, blanch broccoli rabe in large pot of boiling water for 3 minutes. Drain well. Coarsely chop and set aside.

6. Heat olive oil in large nonstick skillet. Add garlic; sauté 1 minute. Add blanched broccoli rabe, salt and pepper; sauté for 2 minutes.

7. Combine Swiss, mozzarella and Parmesan cheeses in small bowl.

8. Sprinkle half of cheese mixture evenly over prebaked crust, leaving ½-inch border all around. Top with broccoli rabe mixture. Arrange tomatoes over top. Sprinkle evenly with remaining cheese mixture.

9. Bake for 8 to 10 minutes, or until cheese is melted, topping is heated through and edge of crust is browned. Let stand 5 minutes before cutting.

Makes 8 slices.

184 CALORIES PER SLICE: 11 G PROTEIN; 5 G FAT; 25 G CARBOHYDRATE; 257 MG SODIUM; 12 MG CHOLESTEROL.

Mexican Pizza With Corn and Chilies

1	recipe Basic Pizza Dough (page 20)
	Yellow cornmeal for pan
1	cup bottled salsa, drained
¼	pound Monterey Jack cheese, shredded (about 1 cup)
½	teaspoon ground cumin
1	can (4 ounces) chopped mild green chilies
1	cup fresh or frozen corn kernels
4	scallions, chopped

1. Prepare Basic Pizza Dough, reserving half the dough for another pizza.

2. Preheat oven to 500 degrees F. Place oven rack in lowest position.

3. Sprinkle bottom of 9-inch-round layer-cake pan with a little cornmeal. Pat dough out evenly in pan, leaving a slight edge all around.

4. Bake crust on lowest oven rack for 7 minutes, or until dough is lightly browned and crisp.

5. Spread salsa evenly over prebaked crust, leaving ½-inch border all around. Sprinkle with cheese, cumin, green chilies, corn and scallions.

6. Bake for 8 to 10 minutes, or until topping is heated through and edge of crust is browned. Let stand for 5 minutes before cutting.

Makes 8 slices.

171 CALORIES PER SLICE: 7 G PROTEIN; 5 G FAT; 25 G CARBOHYDRATE; 379 MG SODIUM; 13 MG CHOLESTEROL.

Shrimp Pizza With Feta

1	recipe Basic Pizza Dough (page 20)
1	cup (½ recipe) Basic Chunky Tomato Sauce (page 23)
	Yellow cornmeal for pan
½	pound medium-size cooked, shelled, deveined shrimp (¾-1 pound uncooked, in shell)
¼	pound feta cheese, crumbled
½	red onion, cut into thin slices and separated into rings
1	teaspoon dried oregano
¼	teaspoon freshly ground black pepper

1. Prepare Basic Pizza Dough, reserving half the dough for another pizza. Prepare Basic Chunky Tomato Sauce.

2. Preheat oven to 500 degrees F. Place oven rack in lowest position.

3. Sprinkle 9-inch-round layer-cake pan or cast-iron skillet with a little cornmeal. Pat dough out evenly in pan, leaving slight edge all around.

4. Bake crust on lowest oven rack for 5 minutes, or until lightly browned and crisp.

5. Spread tomato sauce evenly over prebaked crust, leaving ½-inch border all around. Arrange shrimp over sauce. Sprinkle crumbled feta over shrimp. Scatter red onion rings over all. Sprinkle with oregano and pepper.

6. Bake for 8 to 10 minutes, or until topping is heated through and edge of crust is browned. Let stand for 5 minutes before cutting.

Makes 8 slices.

175 CALORIES PER SLICE: 11 G PROTEIN; 4 G FAT; 23 G CARBOHYDRATE; 403 MG SODIUM; 68 MG CHOLESTEROL.

Eggplant, Basil and Goat Cheese Pie

1	recipe Basic Pizza Dough (page 20)
1	cup (½ recipe) Basic Chunky Tomato Sauce (page 23)
1	small eggplant (¾ pound), sliced ¼ inch thick
½	teaspoon salt
4	cloves garlic, unpeeled
	Yellow cornmeal for pizza pan
½	cup shredded fresh basil leaves
1	tablespoon pine nuts
¼	pound reduced-fat mozzarella cheese, shredded (about 1 cup)
2	tablespoons grated Parmesan cheese
2	ounces fresh goat cheese, crumbled (about ½ cup)

1. Prepare Basic Pizza Dough, reserving half the dough for another pizza. Prepare Basic Chunky Tomato Sauce.

2. Toss eggplant with salt in colander. Place over a bowl or in sink and let stand 30 minutes.

3. Preheat oven to 500 degrees F. Place oven rack in lowest position.

4. Roast garlic cloves in preheated oven in pie tin for 15 to 20 minutes, or until softened. Set aside. Leave oven on.

5. Sprinkle 12-inch pizza pan with a little cornmeal. Pat dough out evenly in pan, leaving slight edge all around.

6. Bake crust on lowest oven rack for 5 minutes, or until lightly browned and crisp.

7. Meanwhile, wipe eggplant dry with paper towels. Steam in steamer rack over boiling water in covered saucepan for 8 to 10 minutes, or until just tender. Drain well on paper towels.

8. Rub prebaked crust with softened roasted garlic; discard papery garlic skin. Spread tomato sauce evenly over crust, leaving ½-inch border all around. Top with eggplant, basil and pine nuts. Sprinkle with mozzarella, Parmesan and goat cheeses.

9. Bake for 8 to 10 minutes, or until topping is heated through and edge of crust is browned. Let stand for 5 minutes before cutting.

Makes 8 slices.

186 CALORIES PER SLICE: 10 G PROTEIN; 6 G FAT; 25 G CARBOHYDRATE; 477 MG SODIUM; 12 MG CHOLESTEROL.

Asparagus, Artichoke and Red Pepper Pizza

1	recipe Basic Pizza Dough (page 20)
1	cup (½ recipe) Basic Chunky Tomato Sauce (page 23)
½	pound fresh asparagus or steamed broccoli florets
1	jar (6 ounces) marinated artichoke hearts, drained, rinsed and patted dry
	Yellow cornmeal for pizza pan
1	red bell pepper, cored, seeded and cut lengthwise into thin strips
¼	pound blue cheese, crumbled (about 1 cup)

1. Prepare Basic Pizza Dough, reserving half the dough for another pizza. Prepare Basic Chunky Tomato Sauce.

2. Preheat oven to 500 degrees F. Place oven rack in lowest position.

3. Bring skillet of water to gentle boil. If using asparagus, snap off tough ends and discard. Rinse asparagus. Place in simmering water and cook until crisp-tender, about 4 minutes. Carefully drain in colander. Rinse under cold water to stop cooking. Pat dry with paper towels.

4. Cut artichoke hearts into small pieces.

5. Sprinkle 12-inch pizza pan with a little cornmeal. Pat dough out evenly in pan, leaving slight edge all around.

6. Bake crust on lowest oven rack for 5 minutes, or until lightly browned and crisp.

7. Spread tomato sauce evenly over prebaked crust, leaving ½-inch border all around. Arrange red pepper over sauce, then artichoke pieces and asparagus or broccoli. Sprinkle evenly with blue cheese.

8. Bake for 8 to 10 minutes, or until topping is heated through and edge of crust is browned. Let stand for 5 minutes before cutting.

Makes 8 slices.

175 CALORIES PER SLICE: 8 G PROTEIN; 5 G FAT; 25 G CARBOHYDRATE; 401 MG SODIUM; 10 MG CHOLESTEROL.

This rich, elegant pizza makes an excellent first course or appetizer pizza for eight, or a light, summer afternoon offering for four (although we've been known to devour one between the two of us). If fresh asparagus is out of season, substitute frozen, cooked according to package directions. A crisp Alsatian Riesling wine is the perfect accompaniment for this pizza. Strawberries, raspberries or blackberries or all three, splashed with a little Champagne, would make a simple but luxurious ending to the meal.

Black Bean Pizza

1   recipe Basic Pizza Dough (page 20)
1   cup Basic Chunky Tomato Sauce (page 23), prepared with
        4 cloves garlic
     Yellow cornmeal for pizza pan
1   can (19 ounces) black beans, drained and rinsed
3   ounces reduced-fat mozzarella cheese, shredded (about ¾ cup)
2   ounces Monterey Jack cheese, shredded (about ½ cup)
2   tablespoons chopped fresh cilantro (optional)

1. Prepare Basic Pizza Dough, reserving half the dough for another pizza. Prepare Basic Chunky Tomato Sauce.

2. Preheat oven to 500 degrees F. Place oven rack in lowest position.

3. Sprinkle 12-inch pizza pan with a little cornmeal. Pat dough out evenly in pan, leaving slight edge all around.

4. Bake crust on lowest oven rack for 5 minutes, or until edge is lightly browned and crisp.

5. Spread tomato sauce evenly over prebaked crust, leaving ½-inch border all around. Top with beans, then cheeses.

6. Bake for 8 to 10 minutes, or until topping is heated through and edge of crust is browned. Sprinkle with cilantro, if using. Let stand for 5 minutes before cutting.

Makes 8 slices.

222 CALORIES PER SLICE: 13 G PROTEIN; 4 G FAT; 33 G CARBOHYDRATE; 291 MG SODIUM; 10 MG CHOLESTEROL.

Chicken Pizza With Three Cheeses

1	recipe Basic Pizza Dough (page 20)
½	pound boneless, skinless chicken breasts
	Juice of 1 lemon
2	teaspoons dried oregano
	Yellow cornmeal for pizza pan
1	tablespoon bottled barbecue sauce
2	ounces Cheddar cheese, shredded (about ½ cup)
1	ounce reduced-fat mozzarella cheese, shredded (about ¼ cup)
1	ounce reduced-fat provolone cheese, shredded (about ¼ cup)
10	scallions, chopped (½ cup)

1. Prepare Basic Pizza Dough, reserving half the dough for another pizza.

2. Meanwhile, combine chicken, lemon juice and oregano in small bowl. Let stand at room temperature for 30 minutes.

3. Preheat broiler. Place chicken on broiler-pan rack.

4. Broil chicken 2 inches from heat for about 3 minutes on each side, or until no longer pink in center. Remove chicken from oven. Lower oven temperature to 500 degrees F. Place oven rack in lowest position. When chicken is cool enough to handle, cut into small dice.

5. Sprinkle 12-inch pizza pan with a little cornmeal. Pat dough out evenly in pan, leaving slight edge all around. Brush barbecue sauce over crust, leaving ½-inch border all around.

6. Bake crust on lowest oven rack for 5 minutes, or until lightly browned and crisp.

(continued on page 48)

7. Combine Cheddar, mozzarella and provolone cheeses in small bowl.

8. Scatter chicken evenly over prebaked crust. Scatter scallions over chicken, followed by cheese mixture.

9. Bake for 8 to 10 minutes, or until cheese is melted, topping is heated through and edge of crust is browned. Let stand for 5 minutes before cutting.

Makes 8 slices.

164 CALORIES PER SLICE: 11 G PROTEIN; 5 G FAT; 20 G CARBOHYDRATE; 145 MG SODIUM; 23 MG CHOLESTEROL.

Salad Pizza

1 recipe Basic Pizza Dough (page 20)
Yellow cornmeal for pizza pan
2 ounces Gruyère cheese, shredded (about ½ cup)
2 ounces reduced-fat mozzarella cheese, shredded (about ½ cup)
2 cups shredded crisp lettuce
1 small ripe tomato, seeded and chopped
2 tablespoons low-fat vinaigrette salad dressing
1 tablespoon grated Parmesan cheese

1. Prepare Basic Pizza Dough, reserving half the dough for another pizza.

2. Preheat oven to 500 degrees F. Place oven rack in lowest position.

3. Sprinkle 12-inch pizza pan with a little cornmeal. Pat dough out evenly in pan, leaving slight edge all around.

4. Bake crust on lowest oven rack for 5 minutes, or until edge is lightly browned and crisp.

5. Combine Gruyère and mozzarella cheeses in small bowl. Sprinkle evenly over prebaked crust, leaving ½-inch border all around.

6. Bake for 8 to 10 minutes, or until cheese is melted and edge of crust is browned.

7. Meanwhile, toss together lettuce, tomato, salad dressing and Parmesan cheese in medium-size bowl. Spread evenly over pie. Cut and serve at once.

Makes 8 slices.

147 CALORIES PER SLICE: 8 G PROTEIN; 4 G FAT; 20 G CARBOHYDRATE; 152 MG SODIUM; 11 MG CHOLESTEROL.

The first place we ever had a salad pizza was in the Bronx. We were hooked after the first bite. What makes it special is the contrast between the cool salad ingredients and the warm melted cheese and bread—a variety of flavors, textures and temperatures in every mouthful. This pizza is best made with a crisp lettuce, such as iceberg or hearts of Romaine. We like Gruyère or Swiss cheese mixed with low-fat mozzarella, but any cheese will work just as well. Serve with soup and you'll need little else for lunch or a light dinner.

Cheese, Onion and Apple Pizza

1   recipe Basic Pizza Dough (page 20)
     Yellow cornmeal for pizza pan
2   apples, cored and thinly sliced
½   small red onion, thinly sliced
3   ounces reduced-fat mozzarella cheese, shredded (about ¾ cup)
2   ounces Cheddar cheese, shredded, or blue cheese, crumbled
     (about ½ cup)

1. Prepare Basic Pizza Dough, reserving half the dough for another pizza.

2. Preheat oven to 500 degrees F. Place oven rack in lowest position.

3. Sprinkle 12-inch pizza pan with a little cornmeal. Pat dough out evenly in pan, leaving slight edge all around.

4. Bake crust on lowest oven rack for 5 minutes, or until lightly browned and crisp.

5. Arrange apple slices in single layer over prebaked crust, overlapping slices slightly and leaving ½-inch border all around. Top with slices of red onion. Combine mozzarella and Cheddar or blue cheeses in small bowl. Sprinkle evenly over top.

6. Bake for 8 to 10 minutes, or until topping is heated through and edge of crust is browned. Let stand for 5 minutes before cutting.

Makes 8 slices.

165 CALORIES PER SLICES: 8 G PROTEIN; 4 G FAT; 25 G CARBOHYDRATE; 150 MG SODIUM; 11 MG CHOLESTEROL.

Filled Spinach Pie
With Peppers

1   recipe Basic Calzone Dough (page 56)
1   cup (½ recipe) Basic Chunky Tomato Sauce (page 23)
4   red or yellow bell peppers or a combination
1   teaspoon olive oil
4   cloves garlic, finely chopped
12   ounces fresh spinach leaves, tough stems removed, leaves well
        washed and coarsely chopped
     Yellow cornmeal for pizza pan
1   cup fresh basil leaves, finely chopped
¼   pound reduced-fat mozzarella cheese, shredded (about 1 cup)
3   ounces fresh goat cheese or feta cheese, crumbled

1. Prepare Calzone Dough and Basic Chunky Tomato Sauce. Divide dough in half evenly. Set aside.

2. Preheat broiler. Arrange peppers in single layer on broiler-pan rack and broil peppers 4 inches from heat, turning frequently, for 20 minutes, or until blackened all over. Transfer peppers to paper bag and close. When cool enough to handle, peel off blackened skins. Rinse, if necessary, to remove any stubborn skins. Blot dry. Cut peppers in half and remove stems and seeds. Slice peppers into thin strips. Set aside.

3. Reduce oven temperature to 500 degrees F. Place oven rack in lowest position.

4. Meanwhile, heat olive oil in large nonstick skillet over medium heat. Add garlic; sauté 1 minute. Add spinach, with any water clinging to leaves, to skillet. Cook, stirring, just until leaves are wilted and all liquid has evaporated, 1 to 2 minutes. Set aside.

5. Sprinkle 12-inch pizza pan with a little cornmeal. Press half of dough evenly in pan, leaving edge of dough slightly overlapping edge of pan. Spread tomato sauce evenly over dough to within 1 inch of edge. Top with spinach mixture, basil and peppers. Sprinkle evenly with mozzarella cheese. Crumble goat cheese or feta over all.

(continued on page 54)

A filled pizza is like a big calzone, and one slice makes a hearty main dish. You can stuff a filled pizza with almost anything—just be sure the filling isn't overly wet, or the crust will become soggy. Filled pizzas travel well because the double crust helps keep the filling in place when you're on the move. If you make this pie on a weekend, leftovers can easily be carried to the office for lunch later in the week. One friend said he prefers to eat the slices cold, like a sandwich, rather than reheat them. This makes an excellent picnic pizza.

Serve this pie with a sliced tomato salad and tossed greens. You can substitute 2 cups of chopped cooked broccoli for the spinach, if you like.

6. Roll remaining dough out to 12-inch circle. Place over top of pie so edges of dough are aligned. Press edges of dough together and under to seal. Prick top crust a few times with fork.

7. Bake on lowest oven rack for 25 to 30 minutes, or until crust is crisp and golden brown. Remove from oven. Let stand for 15 minutes before cutting.

Makes 8 slices.

354 CALORIES PER SLICE: 17 G PROTEIN; 7 G FAT; 57 G CARBOHYDRATE; 550 MG SODIUM; 15 MG CHOLESTEROL.

Calzones

PIZZA DOUGH STUFFED WITH VEGETABLES OR CHEESE or various meats and shaped into a half-moon envelope or pocket is called a calzone. Originally, calzones described something called pant legs, which were long tubes of dough wrapped around sausages. They resembled the baggy pants worn by Neapolitan men—hence the name.

Calzones are sometimes fried, but we bake ours to reduce the amount of fat. Fillings range from sausage and pepper and spinach and feta, to a nontraditional potato, Cheddar and roasted red pepper. For entertaining or appetizer fare, try mini calzones, shaping the dough circles into 3- to 5-inch rounds.

We've developed a calzone dough, a variation of Basic Pizza Dough, with yellow cornmeal for texture and low-fat yogurt, which provides richness without contributing excessive fat. The pizza dough will work equally well.

Calzones are best eaten fresh from the oven, but they can be gently reheated, covered with a paper towel, in a microwave oven for about 30 seconds, or in a 350-degree F oven, covered loosely with aluminum foil, for 15 to 20 minutes. For added pizzazz, serve with Basic Chunky Tomato Sauce (page 23), or its Roasted Red Pepper Variation as a dipping sauce.

Basic Calzone Dough

1	envelope (2½ teaspoons) active dry yeast
2	teaspoons sugar
½	cup lukewarm skim milk (95-105 degrees F)
1	cup low-fat plain yogurt
¼	cup yellow cornmeal
¾	teaspoon salt
3½	cups unbleached all-purpose flour, plus extra for kneading

1. Dissolve yeast and sugar in lukewarm milk in large bowl. Let stand until foamy, 5 to 10 minutes.

2. **Hand method:** Stir in yogurt, cornmeal and salt with your hand or large spoon until well mixed. Stir in flour, 1 cup at a time, mixing thoroughly after each addition, to make soft dough.

Food-processor method: Combine flour, cornmeal and salt in a food processor. Stir together yeast mixture and yogurt in small bowl. With motor running, add yeast-yogurt mixture through feed tube and continue to process just until dough comes together in ball.

3. Turn dough out onto lightly floured work surface. Knead until smooth and elastic, 5 to 10 minutes, adding a little flour as needed to prevent sticking. Cover with inverted bowl. Let rest 10 minutes.

4. Use dough to make calzones or refrigerate or freeze as directed below.

To refrigerate: Place dough in plastic bag, leaving a little room for expansion, seal tightly and refrigerate for up to 3 days. Let come to room temperature before using as directed in recipe.

To freeze: Make dough through Step 3. Divide dough into 6 equal pieces. Knead each piece lightly and shape into a flattened round. Dust with flour or cornmeal, wrap tightly in plastic wrap and freeze. Thaw dough in refrigerator, then let stand at room temperature for 30 minutes before rolling and filling.

Makes enough dough for 6 individual calzones.

326 CALORIES PER PORTION OF CALZONE DOUGH: 11 G PROTEIN; 1 G FAT; 66 G CARBOHYDRATE; 305 MG SODIUM; 3 MG CHOLESTEROL.

Monterey-Mushroom Calzones

Choose flavorful mushrooms, such as shiitakes, chanterelles and morels. Substitute balsamic or red-wine vinegar for the sherry vinegar, if you like. Mild cheeses allow the flavor of the sautéed mushrooms and herbs to come through.

1   recipe Basic Calzone Dough (page 56)
2   teaspoons olive oil
12   ounces wild or button mushrooms, or a combination, cleaned, tough stems removed, caps sliced
3   scallions, thinly sliced
2   cloves garlic, finely chopped
2   teaspoons chopped fresh thyme or ½ teaspoon dried leaf thyme
2   teaspoons sherry-wine vinegar
¼   cup chopped fresh parsley
½   pound reduced-fat mozzarella cheese, shredded (about 2 cups)
¼   pound Monterey Jack cheese, shredded (about 1 cup)

1. Prepare Basic Calzone Dough.

2. Preheat oven to 400 degrees F.

3. Heat olive oil in large nonstick skillet over medium heat. Add mushrooms; sauté for 3 minutes. Add scallions, garlic, thyme and vinegar; cook 2 minutes longer. Remove from heat. Stir in parsley. Set aside to cool slightly.

4. Combine mozzarella and Monterey Jack cheeses in bowl. Add mushroom mixture; toss gently to combine.

5. Shape dough into 12-inch-long log on lightly floured board. Divide into 6 equal pieces. Roll out 1 piece of dough into 8-inch circle. Spread about ⅔ cup of filling over lower half of circle to within 1½ inches of edge. Fold dough over filling. Fold edges up and over together twice. Press firmly to seal. Crimp a decorative edge, if you like. Transfer calzone to baking sheet. Repeat with remaining filling and dough. Prick top of each calzone several times with point of sharp knife.

6. Bake for 20 to 25 minutes, or until heated through and golden brown. Transfer to wire rack and let stand for 15 minutes before serving.

Makes 6 calzones.

509 CALORIES PER CALZONE: 29 G PROTEIN; 13 G FAT; 71 G CARBOHYDRATE; 663 MG SODIUM; 33 MG CHOLESTEROL.

Spinach and Feta Calzones

*J*ust a small amount of feta cheese is necessary to lend a distinct, tangy flavor to this filling. If you like, use feta that's flavored with cracked black pepper. To be sure your spinach is well drained, turn it into a mesh sieve and press with paper towels to remove as much moisture as possible. Serve this calzone with a ripe tomato salad or a side dish of roasted red peppers and cured olives.

1   recipe Basic Calzone Dough (page 56)
2   packages (10 ounces each) frozen chopped spinach, thawed and
        well drained
20   scallions, thinly sliced (1 cup)
¾   pound (1½ cups) reduced-fat ricotta cheese
¼   pound reduced-fat mozzarella cheese, shredded (about 1 cup)
2   ounces feta cheese, crumbled (about ½ cup)
1½   tablespoons chopped fresh dill or 2 teaspoons dried

1. Prepare Basic Calzone Dough.

2. Preheat oven to 400 degrees F.

3. Combine spinach, scallions, ricotta cheese, mozzarella cheese, feta cheese and dill in large bowl.

4. Shape dough into 12-inch-long log on lightly floured board. Divide into 6 equal pieces. Roll out 1 piece of dough into 8-inch circle. Spread about ¾ cup of spinach filling over lower half of round to within 1½ inches of edge. Fold dough over filling. Fold edges up and over together twice. Press firmly to seal. Crimp a decorative edge, if you like. Transfer calzone to baking sheet. Repeat with remaining filling and dough. Prick top of each calzone several times with point of sharp knife.

5. Bake for 20 to 25 minutes, or until heated through and golden brown. Transfer to wire rack and let stand for 15 minutes before serving.

Makes 6 calzones.

498 CALORIES PER CALZONE: 28 G PROTEIN; 10 G FAT; 75 G CARBOHYDRATE; 689 MG SODIUM; 35 MG CHOLESTEROL.

Sausage and Pepper Calzones

1	cup (½ recipe) Basic Chunky Tomato Sauce (page 23)
1	recipe Basic Calzone Dough (page 56)
1	large onion, thinly sliced
2	green bell peppers, cored, seeded and thinly sliced
2	cloves garlic, finely chopped
2	tablespoons water
4	ounces lean sweet or hot turkey sausages, thinly sliced
½	pound reduced-fat mozzarella cheese, shredded (about 2 cups)
¼	pound provolone cheese, shredded (about 1 cup)

1. Prepare Basic Chunky Tomato Sauce and Basic Calzone Dough.

2. Lightly coat large nonstick skillet with vegetable-oil cooking spray. Heat skillet over medium-low heat. Add onion; sauté 1 minute. Add peppers and garlic; sauté 1 minute. Add water; simmer, stirring, for 2 minutes, or until liquid evaporates. Remove vegetables with slotted spoon to bowl.

3. Wipe out skillet and lightly coat again with cooking spray. Heat over medium heat. Add sausages; cook for 5 minutes, or until browned on all sides. If sausage casings begin to separate from sausage and curl up, remove as necessary. Stir in tomato sauce. Add vegetables back to skillet. Cover and cook 5 minutes, or until meat is cooked through. Set filling aside for 5 minutes.

4. Preheat oven to 400 degrees F.

5. Shape dough into 12-inch-long log on lightly floured board. Divide into 6 equal pieces. Roll out each piece of dough into 8-inch circle. Divide sausage and pepper filling evenly among rounds, spreading over lower half of each round to within 1½ inches of edge.

(continued on page 62)

6. Combine mozzarella and provolone cheeses in small bowl. Sprinkle evenly over filling for each calzone, dividing equally. Fold dough over filling. Fold edges up and over together twice. Press firmly to seal. Crimp a decorative edge, if you like. Transfer calzones to baking sheet. Prick top of each calzone several times with point of sharp knife.

7. Bake for 20 to 25 minutes, or until heated through and golden brown. Transfer to wire rack and let stand for 15 minutes before serving.

Makes 6 calzones.

539 CALORIES PER CALZONE: 33 G PROTEIN; 12 G FAT; 76 G CARBOHYDRATE; 1,081 MG SODIUM; 41 MG CHOLESTEROL.

Chicken Calzones With Mozzarella and Sun-Dried Tomatoes

¼ cup dry-pack sun-dried tomatoes (not packed in oil)
½ cup hot water
1 recipe Basic Calzone Dough (page 56)
3 cups shredded cooked chicken (1 pound uncooked boneless, skinless chicken breasts)
½ pound fresh goat cheese, crumbled
¼ pound reduced-fat mozzarella cheese, shredded (about 1 cup)
½ cup finely chopped fresh parsley or fresh oregano
½ teaspoon salt
¼ teaspoon freshly ground black pepper

1. Soak tomatoes in hot water until soft, about 15 minutes.

2. Meanwhile, prepare Basic Calzone Dough.

3. Drain tomatoes and chop them. Combine chicken, goat cheese, mozzarella cheese, tomatoes, parsley or oregano, salt and pepper in medium-size bowl. You should have about 5 cups filling.

4. Preheat oven to 400 degrees F.

5. Shape dough into 12-inch-long log on lightly floured board. Divide into 6 equal pieces. Roll out 1 piece of dough into 8-inch circle. Spread generous ¾ cup chicken filling over lower half of round to within 1½ inches of edge. Fold dough over filling. Fold edges up and over together twice. Press firmly to seal. Crimp a decorative edge, if you like. Transfer calzone to baking sheet. Repeat with remaining filling and dough. Prick top of each calzone several times with point of sharp knife.

6. Bake for 20 to 25 minutes, or until heated through and golden brown. Transfer to wire rack and let stand for 15 minutes before serving.

Makes 6 calzones.

570 CALORIES PER CALZONE: 37 G PROTEIN; 16 G FAT; 69 G CARBOHYDRATE; 880 MG SODIUM; 69 MG CHOLESTEROL.

The sharpness of sun-dried tomato and the parsley nicely complement the goat cheese and mozzarella in this calzone. To use as an appetizer or as part of the menu for a larger dinner party, try this presentation: Roll out the dough into a 12-inch circle. Spread the filling over half the dough, leaving a 1½-inch border, and fold the other half over. Seal and bake as you would individual calzones. Cut in half with a serrated knife, and then crosswise into 1-inch-wide pieces. You can use leftover cooked chicken, or even deli chicken, with the skin removed.

Spinach and Ricotta Calzones With Raisins

1	recipe Basic Calzone Dough (page 56)
¼-½	cup raisins
1	teaspoon olive oil
6	cloves garlic, crushed through garlic press or finely chopped
2	packages (10 ounces each) frozen spinach or kale, thawed according to package directions and squeezed dry with paper towels
¾	pound (1½ cups) reduced-fat ricotta cheese
½	teaspoon grated nutmeg
½	teaspoon ground cinnamon

1. Prepare Basic Calzone Dough.

2. Soak raisins in small bowl in enough warm water to cover until softened, about 30 minutes.

3. Heat olive oil in large nonstick skillet over medium heat. Add garlic; sauté 30 seconds. Add spinach or kale; cook, covered, stirring occasionally, until slightly tender, about 5 minutes. Remove from heat and place in medium-size bowl.

4. Drain raisins and add to spinach or kale mixture. Stir ricotta cheese, raisins, nutmeg and cinnamon into spinach until well blended.

5. Preheat oven to 400 degrees F.

6. Shape dough into 12-inch-long log on lightly floured board. Divide into 6 equal pieces. Roll out 1 piece of dough into 8-inch circle. Spread about ⅔ cup spinach filling over lower half of round to within 1½ inches of edge. Fold dough over filling. Fold edges up and over together

The flavors in this calzone borrow from Sicilian cooking. The size is ideal for a light supper or lunch, or thinly slice each calzone crosswise with a serrated knife for appetizer-size portions. The filling works equally well with fresh or frozen kale, mustard greens or escarole.

Adding the smaller quantity of raisins yields a slightly less sweet result. For a heartier version, add ¾ cup diced cooked ham to the filling.

twice. Press firmly to seal. Crimp a decorative edge, if you like. Transfer calzone to baking sheet. Repeat with remaining filling and dough. Prick top of each calzone several times with point of sharp knife.

7. Bake for 20 to 25 minutes, or until heated through and golden brown. Transfer to wire rack and let stand for 15 minutes before serving.

Makes 6 calzones.

468 CALORIES PER CALZONE: 22 G PROTEIN; 7 G FAT; 80 G CARBOHYDRATE; 464 MG SODIUM; 22 MG CHOLESTEROL.

This recipe was developed by one of our friends, Craig Hohl, who is a computer expert by day and an apprentice calzone cook by night. These calzones are pleasantly mild in flavor and easy to make because the filling doesn't have to be precooked.

Artichoke and Olive Calzones

1	recipe Basic Calzone Dough (page 56)
1	package (9 ounces) frozen artichoke hearts, thawed and coarsely chopped
2	medium-size ripe tomatoes, cored, seeded and finely chopped (1 cup)
6	scallions, chopped (⅓ cup)
¼	cup canned black olives, drained, rinsed and chopped
¼	cup pimiento-stuffed green olives, chopped
¼	teaspoon salt
⅛	teaspoon freshly ground black pepper
½	pound reduced-fat mozzarella cheese, shredded (about 2 cups)
¼	pound reduced-fat Swiss cheese, shredded (about 1 cup)

1. Prepare Basic Calzone Dough.

2. Preheat oven to 400 degrees F.

3. Combine artichokes, tomatoes, scallions, black and green olives, salt and pepper in large bowl. Add mozzarella and Swiss cheeses.

4. Shape dough into 12-inch-long log. Divide into 6 equal pieces. Roll out 1 piece of dough into 8-inch circle. Spread about 1 cup artichoke filling over lower half of round to within 1½ inches of edge. Fold dough over filling. Fold edges up and over together twice. Press firmly to seal. Crimp a decorative edge, if you like. Transfer calzone to baking sheet. Repeat with remaining filling and dough. Prick top of each calzone several times with point of sharp knife.

5. Bake for 20 to 25 minutes, or until heated through and golden brown. Transfer to wire rack and let stand for 15 minutes before serving.

Makes 6 calzones.

509 CALORIES PER CALZONE: 32 G PROTEIN; 11 G FAT; 74 G CARBOHYDRATE; 857 MG SODIUM; 27 MG CHOLESTEROL.

Make these in springtime when fresh asparagus is at its best and most abundant. Cheddar cheese can be substituted for the Gruyère, if you wish, and you can also experiment with flavored mustards.

Asparagus and Gruyère Calzones

1	recipe Basic Calzone Dough (page 56)
2	pounds fresh asparagus, trimmed, and if necessary, peeled, or broccoli; sliced in 1½-inch lengths
1	tablespoon Dijon mustard
1	teaspoon fresh lemon juice
½	pound reduced-fat mozzarella cheese, shredded (about 2 cups)
¼	pound Gruyère cheese, shredded (about 1 cup)
2	tablespoons grated Parmesan cheese

1. Prepare Basic Calzone Dough.

2. Preheat oven to 400 degrees F.

3. Steam asparagus over boiling water in covered saucepan for 4 to 5 minutes, or until tender. Toss with mustard and lemon juice in large bowl. Add mozzarella, Gruyère and Parmesan cheeses.

4. Shape dough into 12-inch-long log on lightly floured board. Divide into 6 equal pieces. Roll out 1 piece of dough into 8-inch circle. Spread about ¾ cup asparagus filling over lower half of round to within 1½ inches of edge. Fold dough over filling. Fold edges up and over together twice. Press firmly to seal. Crimp a decorative edge, if you like. Transfer calzone to baking sheet. Repeat with remaining filling and dough. Prick top of each calzone several times with point of sharp knife.

5. Bake for 20 to 25 minutes, or until heated through and golden brown. Transfer to wire rack and let stand for 15 minutes before serving.

Makes 6 calzones.

531 CALORIES PER CALZONE: 33 G PROTEIN; 13 G FAT; 73 G CARBOHYDRATE; 700 MG SODIUM; 38 MG CHOLESTEROL.

Cabbage, Carrot and Caraway Calzones

1	recipe Basic Calzone Dough (page 56)
2	teaspoons vegetable oil
1	large onion, finely chopped
1	carrot, pared and chopped
3	cups shredded green cabbage
2	teaspoons caraway seeds
1½	teaspoons Dijon mustard
¼	teaspoon salt
⅛	teaspoon freshly ground black pepper
¼	pound reduced-fat mozzarella cheese, shredded (about 1 cup)
¼	pound Swiss cheese, shredded (about 1 cup)

1. Prepare Basic Calzone Dough.

2. Preheat oven to 400 degrees F.

3. Heat vegetable oil in large nonstick skillet over medium heat. Add onion; sauté 1 minute. Add carrot; sauté 3 minutes. Stir in cabbage, caraway seeds, mustard, salt and pepper. Cover; reduce heat to low and cook for 10 minutes, or until cabbage is wilted, adding water if necessary to prevent sticking. Uncover and cook, stirring, for 1 minute longer. Set aside to cool slightly. Stir in mozzarella and Swiss cheeses just before filling calzones.

4. Shape dough into 12-inch-long log on lightly floured board. Divide into 6 equal pieces. Roll out 1 piece of dough into 8-inch circle. Spread about ¾ cup cabbage filling over lower half of round to within 1½ inches of edge. Fold dough over filling. Fold edges up and over together twice. Press firmly to seal. Crimp a decorative edge, if you like. Transfer calzone to baking sheet. Repeat with remaining filling and dough. Prick top of each calzone several times with point of sharp knife.

5. Bake for 20 to 25 minutes, or until heated through and golden brown. Transfer to wire rack and let stand for 15 minutes before serving.

Makes 6 calzones.

480 CALORIES PER CALZONE: 24 G PROTEIN; 10 G FAT; 73 G CARBOHYDRATE; 600 MG SODIUM; 27 MG CHOLESTEROL.

The flavor of this calzone is reminiscent of a Reuben sandwich, minus the meat. Season the filling with a tablespoon of prepared horseradish instead of or in addition to the mustard, if you like.

Potato, Cheddar and Roasted Red Pepper Calzones

1½	pounds red-skinned potatoes, peeled and cut into ½-inch dice
1	recipe Basic Calzone Dough (page 56)
¼	pound sharp Cheddar cheese, shredded (about 1 cup)
20	scallions, chopped (1 cup)
½	cup chopped bottled roasted red pepper, drained
1	teaspoon ground cumin
¼	teaspoon salt
¼	teaspoon freshly ground black pepper

1. Preheat oven to 400 degrees F.

2. Lightly grease nonstick baking pan. Spread potatoes in single layer in pan.

3. Bake potatoes for 30 to 45 minutes, or until dark golden brown and crisp, turning every 10 minutes. Leave oven at 400 degrees.

4. Meanwhile, prepare Basic Calzone Dough.

5. Combine potatoes, Cheddar cheese, scallions, roasted red pepper, cumin, salt and pepper in medium-size bowl.

6. Shape dough into 12-inch-long log on lightly floured board. Divide into 6 equal pieces. Roll out 1 piece of dough into 8-inch circle. Spread generous ½ cup potato mixture over lower half of round to within 1½ inches of edge. Fold dough over potato filling. Fold edges up and over together twice. Press firmly to seal. Crimp a decorative edge if you like. Transfer calzone to baking sheet. Repeat with remaining filling and dough. Prick top of each calzone several times with point of sharp knife.

7. Bake for 20 to 25 minutes, or until heated through and golden brown. Transfer to wire rack and let stand for 15 minutes before serving.

Makes 6 calzones.

505 CALORIES PER CALZONE: 18 G PROTEIN; 8 G FAT; 90 G CARBOHYDRATE; 518 MG SODIUM; 23 MG CHOLESTEROL.

Crostini

TOAST WITH A TOPPING—that's probably the simplest definition of crostini. Italian versions frequently use coarse bread, topped with such combinations as seasoned chopped chicken livers; tomatoes, olive oil and garlic; or mozzarella and anchovy. The variations are endless. Our toppings range from chilied corn with cilantro, sweet red pepper with black olives, to caramelized onion, and smoked salmon spread.

These are the easiest hors d'oeuvres to prepare, especially when the topping is a no-cook assembly, such as mushroom with Parmesan (page 77). What bread to use is really your choice, although the size of the slice should be kept small.

When your grill is in operation during the summer, toast the bread over charcoal for a more intense flavor.

Several crostini paired with soup make an easy lunch or light supper, and all of our toppings easily transform into tempting sandwich fillers.

Crostini Toasts

16 slices bread (3 inches wide, ¼ inch thick)
1 clove garlic, crushed (optional)

1. Preheat oven to 350 degrees F.

2. Arrange bread in single layer on baking sheet.

3. Bake for about 10 minutes, or until crisp and lightly browned. Rub browned side lightly with garlic, if you like.

Makes 16 crostini toasts.

25 CALORIES PER TOAST: 1 G PROTEIN; 0 G FAT; 4 G CARBOHYDRATE; 48 MG SODIUM; 0 MG CHOLESTEROL.

Practically any type of bread can be used for crostini, from whole-wheat to plain white. We prefer to keep the slices about ¼ inch thick and no more than about 3 inches wide. Small baguettes are the perfect size. For a slightly different shape, slice the bread diagonally to form exaggerated ovals. If you have only a store-bought rectangular loaf in the house, use 4 slices and cut diagonally from corner to corner to make 4 equal triangles.

Traditionally, the bread is brushed with olive oil before toasting, a step we've omitted to reduce fat. The toasts can be made a few days ahead and kept at room temperature in an airtight container. If you like, recrisp the crostini in a preheated 350-degree oven for a minute or two.

Roasted Sweet Pepper Crostini With Black Olives

1 recipe Crostini Toasts (page 73)
2 red bell peppers
1 teaspoon olive oil
¼ cup finely chopped onion
2 cloves garlic, finely chopped
¼ teaspoon salt
⅛ teaspoon freshly ground black pepper
¼ cup canned black olives, drained and finely chopped
2 tablespoons grated Parmesan cheese
1 tablespoon finely chopped fresh parsley

1. Prepare Crostini Toasts.

2. Preheat broiler. Broil peppers on broiler-pan rack 4 inches from heat, turning frequently, for about 20 minutes, or until blackened on all sides. Transfer peppers to small paper bag and close. Set aside for 15 minutes. Leave broiler on.

3. Meanwhile, heat olive oil in small nonstick skillet. Add onion; sauté for 3 minutes. Add garlic, salt and pepper; sauté 1 minute longer. Remove from heat and set aside.

4. When peppers are cool enough to handle, peel off blackened skins. Rinse, if necessary, to remove any stubborn skins. Blot dry. Core, seed and finely chop peppers. Combine peppers, olives and onion mixture in small bowl.

5. Spread about 1 tablespoon pepper mixture evenly over each toast. Combine cheese and parsley in small bowl. Sprinkle over crostini. Arrange crostini in single layer on baking sheet.

6. Broil crostini 4 inches from heat for 30 to 60 seconds, or until cheese is just barely melted. Serve warm.

Makes 16 crostini.

38 CALORIES PER CROSTINI: 1 G PROTEIN; 1 G FAT; 5 G CARBOHYDRATE; 108 MG SODIUM; 1 MG CHOLESTEROL.

Use red, yellow, orange or green bell peppers, or a combination. This topping is quite flavorful made with canned California black olives, but cured Mediterranean olives add a more authentic and intense taste. A tablespoonful of chopped fresh basil can also be added to the pepper mixture.

Inspired by a combination of Middle Eastern flavors, this crostini recipe marries the sweetness of chutney with the sharpness of oregano and eggplant. The eggplant mixture can be made a day ahead and refrigerated, but for maximum flavor, let it come to room temperature before using.

Eggplant Crostini With Provolone

1	recipe Crostini Toasts (page 73)
1	small eggplant (½ pound), trimmed and sliced crosswise ¼ inch thick
¼	cup chopped fresh oregano or 1 tablespoon dried
3-4	tablespoons chutney, finely chopped
3	ounces provolone cheese, shredded (about ¾ cup)

1. Prepare Crostini Toasts.

2. Preheat oven to 350 degrees F. Arrange eggplant slices in single layer on baking sheet. Bake eggplant for 10 minutes on each side, or until tender. Increase oven temperature to broil.

3. Cut eggplant into ¼-inch dice. Gently mix with oregano in bowl.

4. Spread each toast with ½ teaspoon chutney. Top chutney with 1 tablespoon eggplant, spreading gently. Sprinkle each with 1 teaspoon packed shredded provolone. Arrange crostini on baking sheet.

5. Broil 4 inches from heat for 30 seconds, or until cheese is melted. Serve immediately.

Makes 16 crostini.

55 CALORIES PER CROSTINI: 2 G PROTEIN; 2 G FAT; 7 G CARBOHYDRATE; 96 MG SODIUM; 4 MG CHOLESTEROL.

Mushroom Crostini With Parmesan

1	recipe Crostini Toasts (page 73)
¼	pound button mushrooms, wiped clean and tough stems trimmed
1	ounce Parmesan, Pecorino Romano or Asiago cheese
2½	tablespoons Dijon mustard
½	lemon
	Freshly ground black pepper

1. Prepare Crostini Toasts.

2. Slice mushrooms as thinly as possible. Shave cheese thinly with swivel-bladed vegetable peeler.

3. Spread each toast with a scant ½ teaspoon mustard. Layer mushroom slices on toast, about 4 slices per toast. Sprinkle each with few drops lemon juice. Cover with 2 or 3 shavings of cheese. Top each with a grinding or two of pepper. Serve.

Makes 16 crostini.

37 CALORIES PER CROSTINI: 2 G PROTEIN; 1 G FAT; 5 G CARBOHYDRATE; 113 MG SODIUM; 1 MG CHOLESTEROL.

This crostini has pure mushroom flavor. There's no cooking here, just some quick preparation and assembling. Make sure the mushrooms are as fresh as possible, and the better the quality of the cheese, the better the flavor of the crostini will be.

Caramelized Onion Crostini

1   recipe Crostini Toasts (page 73)
2   teaspoons olive oil
1½ pounds yellow onions, chopped (about 3 large onions)
⅛   teaspoon salt
    Pinch freshly ground black pepper
2   tablespoons sugar
¼   cup dry red wine
1   tablespoon balsamic vinegar
1   tablespoon chopped fresh parsley

1. Prepare Crostini Toasts.

2. Heat olive oil in large nonstick skillet over medium heat. Stir in onions, salt and pepper. Reduce heat to low; cover and cook for 20 minutes, stirring occasionally.

3. Uncover skillet. Sprinkle onions with sugar; stir well. Cook, uncovered, for 10 minutes. Stir in wine and vinegar; cook, stirring occasionally, for 30 minutes longer, or until mixture is soft and thick. Remove from heat. Stir in parsley.

4. Spoon about 1 tablespoon topping over each toast. Serve warm or at room temperature.

Makes 16 crostini.

55 CALORIES PER CROSTINI: 1 G PROTEIN; 1 G FAT; 10 G CARBOHYDRATE; 67 MG SODIUM; 0 MG CHOLESTEROL.

This sweet, thick topping has a rich, winey flavor and a marmalade-like consistency. A little goes a long way. If you like, smear the toast with low-fat cream cheese before topping with caramelized onions. The onion mixture can be made a day ahead and refrigerated, but wait to mix in the parsley until just before serving.

Tomato and Broccoli Crostini With Basil

We left this topping cheeseless. You could, however, add a sprinkling of grated Asiago or Parmesan and then lightly broil to melt the cheese just before serving.

1   recipe Crostini Toasts (page 73)
2   teaspoons olive oil
¼   cup finely chopped onion
2   cloves garlic, finely chopped
1   cup very finely chopped broccoli or half a 10-ounce package
        frozen chopped broccoli, thawed and drained
¼   teaspoon salt
    Pinch freshly ground black pepper
1   medium-size ripe tomato, cored, seeded and finely chopped
1   tablespoon chopped fresh basil or 1 teaspoon dried

1. Prepare Crostini Toasts.

2. Heat olive oil in medium-size nonstick skillet over medium heat. Add onion; sauté for 3 minutes. Add garlic; sauté for 1 minute. Add broccoli, salt and pepper (add dried basil now, if using); sauté 2 minutes. Stir in tomato; cook for 2 minutes longer. Remove from heat. Stir in fresh basil, if using.

3. Spread about 1 tablespoon topping over each toast. Serve warm.

Makes 16 crostini.

34 CALORIES PER CROSTINI: 1 G PROTEIN; 1 G FAT; 5 G CARBOHYDRATE; 84 MG SODIUM; 0 MG CHOLESTEROL.

Crostini With White Beans and Rosemary

1 recipe Crostini Toasts (page 73)

1 recipe Crostini Toasts (page 73)
3 scallions, trimmed and sliced
1 can (19 ounces) cannellini beans, drained and rinsed
1 tablespoon balsamic vinegar
2 teaspoons olive oil
¼ teaspoon dried rosemary, crumbled
¼ teaspoon salt
⅛ teaspoon freshly ground black pepper

1. Prepare Crostini Toasts.

2. Place scallions in food processor. Whirl until chopped. Add beans, vinegar, oil, rosemary, salt and pepper. Whirl until well combined. Refrigerate, covered, for up to 3 days.

3. Spread about 1½ tablespoons topping on each toast.

Makes 16 crostini.

69 CALORIES PER CROSTINI: 3 G PROTEIN; 1 G FAT; 12 G CARBOHYDRATE; 232 MG SODIUM; 0 MG CHOLESTEROL.

Garnish these crostini with a little chopped parsley, a small sliver of baked or smoked ham, or very thin slices of plum tomato. This bean spread is a great sandwich filler with roasted red peppers or thinly sliced ham.

Artichoke and Tomato Crostini

1	recipe Crostini Toasts (page 73)
1	teaspoon olive oil
½	cup finely chopped onion (½ small onion)
½	teaspoon ground cumin
½	teaspoon paprika
¼	teaspoon salt
½	9-ounce package frozen artichoke hearts, cooked according to package directions
1	small ripe plum tomato, cored, seeded and finely chopped
¼	cup canned black olives, drained, rinsed and finely chopped
1	tablespoon low-fat plain yogurt
2	teaspoons fresh lemon juice
1	tablespoon chopped fresh cilantro or parsley
	Fresh cilantro or parsley for garnish (optional)

1. Prepare Crostini Toasts.

2. Heat olive oil in small nonstick skillet over medium heat. Add onion, cumin, paprika and salt; sauté 3 minutes, or until onion is tender.

3. Finely chop artichokes. Combine artichokes, onion mixture, tomato, olives, yogurt, lemon juice and cilantro or parsley in small bowl.

4. Spread about 1 tablespoon topping over each toast slice. Garnish with cilantro or parsley, if you like.

Makes 16 crostini.

38 CALORIES PER CROSTINI: 1 G PROTEIN; 1 G FAT; 6 G CARBOHYDRATE; 102 MG SODIUM; 0 MG CHOLESTEROL.

Sweet, toasty cumin and a hint of yogurt give this topping its Middle Eastern flavor. Render it Italian by substituting equal amounts of dried oregano and basil for the cumin and paprika, omitting the yogurt and using Italian-style cured olives and flat-leaf parsley.

Crostini With Smoked Salmon

1	recipe Crostini Toasts (page 73)
½	cup reduced-fat or nonfat cottage cheese
2	ounces Neufchâtel cheese (light cream cheese)
2	ounces sliced smoked salmon
1	tablespoon fresh lemon juice
1	tablespoon chopped fresh dill
1	teaspoon bottled horseradish
⅛	teaspoon freshly ground black pepper

1. Prepare Crostini Toasts.

2. Combine cottage cheese and Neufchâtel cheese in food processor. Whirl until smooth, about 1 minute. Add salmon, lemon juice, dill, horseradish and pepper. Whirl until well mixed. Refrigerate, covered, until ready to use.

3. Spread 1 tablespoon of the salmon mixture over each toast.

Makes 16 crostini.

42 CALORIES PER CROSTINI: 3 G PROTEIN; 1 G FAT; 5 G CARBOHYDRATE; 128 MG SODIUM; 2 MG CHOLESTEROL.

Strongly flavored, these crostini feature the classic combination of smoked salmon and dill, mixed with two reduced-fat cheeses. Garnish the toasts with a small sliver of smoked salmon and a fresh dill sprig. The salmon mixture is also delicious as a filling for cherry tomatoes or spread on cucumber rounds or radishes.

Chilied Corn Crostini

A combination of chili powder, cumin and cinnamon seasons these toasts with sweet Southwestern flavor. For a little heat, add a teaspoon of finely chopped pickled jalapeño peppers or a dash of hot sauce.

1	recipe Crostini Toasts (page 73)
2	teaspoons olive oil
¼	cup finely chopped red bell pepper
1	teaspoon chili powder
½	teaspoon ground cumin
¼	teaspoon ground cinnamon
¼	teaspoon salt
1	cup fresh corn kernels or half a 10-ounce package frozen corn kernels, thawed and drained
½	cup finely chopped, seeded tomato
1	tablespoon finely chopped fresh cilantro
1	scallion, finely chopped

1. Prepare Crostini Toasts.

2. Heat olive oil in medium-size nonstick skillet over medium heat. Add red pepper; sauté for 1 minute. Add chili powder, cumin, cinnamon and salt; sauté for 3 minutes. Stir in corn and tomato; cook until mixture is heated through. Remove from heat. Stir in cilantro and scallion.

3. Spoon about 1 tablespoon topping on each toast. Serve warm.

Makes 16 crostini.

39 CALORIES PER CROSTINI: 1 G PROTEIN; 1 G FAT; 7 G CARBOHYDRATE; 84 MG SODIUM; 0 MG CHOLESTEROL.

This topping has a slight sweet-and-sour flavor. It can be served as a side dish for two to go along with a pork or poultry main dish. It can also be used as a filling for omelets.

Sweet Red Pepper Crostini With Spinach

1 recipe Crostini Toasts (page 73)
1 teaspoon olive oil
½ large onion, finely chopped (½ cup)
2 cloves garlic, finely chopped
¼ cup finely chopped red bell pepper
½ pound fresh spinach, trimmed of tough stems and coarsely chopped, or 1 package (10 ounces) frozen spinach, thawed, squeezed dry
¼ teaspoon salt
⅛ teaspoon freshly ground black pepper
Pinch grated nutmeg
¼ cup water
2 teaspoons red-wine vinegar
3 tablespoons grated Parmesan cheese

1. Prepare Crostini Toasts.

2. Heat olive oil in large nonstick skillet over medium heat. Add onion; sauté 3 minutes. Add garlic; sauté 1 minute. Add red pepper; sauté for 3 minutes longer.

3. Stir in spinach, salt, pepper and nutmeg; cook, stirring, for 3 minutes. Continue cooking, adding water if fresh spinach is used, 1 tablespoon at a time at 5-minute intervals, for about 10 minutes, or until spinach is tender. Stir in vinegar; cook for 1 minute longer.

4. Preheat broiler.

5. Spoon about 1 tablespoon spinach topping on each toast. Sprinkle each with about ½ teaspoon Parmesan. Arrange crostini on baking sheet.

6. Broil crostini 4 inches from heat for 30 seconds, or just until cheese is barely melted. Serve warm.

Makes 16 crostini.

38 CALORIES PER CROSTINI: 2 G PROTEIN; 1 G FAT; 6 G CARBOHYDRATE; 111 MG SODIUM; 1 MG CHOLESTEROL.

Crostini With Deviled Clams

1   recipe Crostini Toasts (page 73)
1   teaspoon olive oil
3   scallions, chopped
1   clove garlic, chopped
2   cans (6½ ounces each) minced clams, drained and blotted dry
        on paper towels
2   teaspoons Dijon mustard
1   teaspoon fresh lemon juice
¼   teaspoon dried oregano
¼   teaspoon salt
⅛   teaspoon freshly ground black pepper
1-2   dashes hot-pepper sauce

The inspiration for this crostini is the seaside favorite, steamed clams oreganata—oregano, mustard and a little hot-pepper sauce. The topping can be made earlier in the day and served cold, or it can be gently reheated in a skillet and then spooned on the crostini. Garnish with little slivers of lemon zest or chopped parsley, or both.

1. Prepare Crostini Toast.

2. Heat olive oil in medium-size nonstick skillet over medium-low heat. Add scallions, sauté over medium-low heat until softened, 2 to 3 minutes. Add garlic; sauté for 30 seconds. Add clams, mustard, lemon juice, oregano, salt, pepper and hot-pepper sauce; gently heat through, 2 to 3 minutes.

3. Spoon generous 2 teaspoons clam topping on each toast. Serve. Or refrigerate clam topping for up to 1 day, and serve cold on crostini or gently reheat. The crostini, covered with a paper towel, can be heated in a microwave oven at 70 percent power for 5 seconds.

Makes 16 crostini.

60 CALORIES PER CROSTINI: 6 G PROTEIN; 1 G FAT; 6 G CARBOHYDRATE; 114 MG SODIUM; 14 MG CHOLESTEROL.

Gazpacho Crostini

1	recipe Crostini Toasts (page 73)
1	cup peeled, diced cucumber
½	diced red or green bell pepper
½	cup diced, seeded, drained tomato, fresh or canned
2	scallions, chopped
2	tablespoons chopped fresh cilantro or parsley
1	clove garlic, crushed through garlic press or finely chopped
¼	cup bottled nonfat Italian salad dressing
1	teaspoon red-wine vinegar
2-3	dashes hot-pepper sauce
½	teaspoon salt
¼	teaspoon freshly ground black pepper

1. Prepare Crostini Toasts.

2. Combine cucumber, bell pepper, tomato, scallions, cilantro or parsley, garlic, salad dressing, vinegar, hot-pepper sauce and salt and pepper in medium-size bowl. Let stand at room temperature for 1 to 2 hours.

3. Heap generous tablespoon of tomato mixture on each toast.

Makes 16 crostini.

29 CALORIES PER CROSTINI: 1 G PROTEIN; 0 G FAT; 6 G CARBOHYDRATE; 124 MG SODIUM; 0 MG CHOLESTEROL.

All the elements of gazpacho: cucumber, tomato, bell pepper, vinegar—but no oil. For best flavor, let stand at room temperature an hour or two. The idea for this combination came from long-time friend John Leo, during a rambling conversation about crostini late one evening.

Pear and Watercress Crostini

1 recipe Crostini Toasts (page 73)
4 ounces gorgonzola or blue cheese, crumbled
1 ripe Bosc pear, quartered, seeded, and each quarter cut
    lengthwise into 8 thin slices
½ bunch watercress, arugula or flat-leaf Italian parsley or cilantro,
    tough stems removed

1. Prepare Crostini Toasts.

2. Preheat broiler.

3. Spread 1½ teaspoons cheese on each toast. Top each with 2 slices of pear. Arrange crostini on baking sheet.

4. Broil crostini about 4 inches from heat until cheese is warm, about 10 to 15 seconds. Let cool slightly. Garnish with watercress, arugula, parsley or cilantro leaves.

Makes 16 crostini.

55 CALORIES PER CROSTINI: 2 G PROTEIN; 2 G FAT; 6 G CARBOHYDRATE; 148 MG SODIUM; 5 MG CHOLESTEROL.

We've adapted the traditional combination of fruit and cheese for this crostini, which works equally well with slices of apple in place of the pear. The sharp flavor of watercress is a good match for the sweet pear and pungent cheese. Serve with French onion soup or potato chowder for a fireside supper. For an almost-dessert version, use 4 slices of raisin-cinnamon bread for the crostini.

Index